Venus

Ray Spangenburg and Kit Moser

Franklin Watts
A Division of Scholastic Inc.
New York • Toronto • London • Auckland • Sydney
Mexico City • New Delhi • Hong Kong
Danbury, Connecticut

For Alex, Alexa, Ashli, Emily, Gabrielle, Heather (Roo),
Joseph, Joyanna, Nick, and Morgan

Note to readers: Definitions for words in **bold** can be found in the Glossary at the back of this book.

Photographs ©: Corbis-Bettmann: 15; Finley-Holiday Films: 6 (3.Creation); Liaison Agency, Inc.: 50 (Bob Stern); NASA: 33, 36, 40, 49, (JPL), 3 left, 20, 21, 25, 28, 34, 42, 43, 44, 46; Photo Researchers: cover (Mark Marten/NASA), 30 (NASA/SS), 29 (NASA/SPL), 4 (Pekka Parviainen/SPL), 10, 11 (Ludek Pesek/SPL), 3 right, 8, 38, 39, 48 (NASA/ SS); Smithsonian Institution, Washington, DC: 23; Sovfoto/Eastfoto: 24 (Itar-Tass), 27 (Tass), 18, 22, 32; Yerkes Observatory: 12.

Solar system diagram created by Greg Harris

Visit Franklin Watts on the Internet at:
http://publishing.grolier.com

Library of Congress Cataloging-in-Publication Data

Spangenburg, Ray, 1939–
    Venus/ Ray Spangenburg and Kit Moser.
      p.   cm.— (Watts Library)
    Includes bibliographical references and index.
    ISBN: 0-531-11768-5 (lib. bdg.)   0-531-13992-1 (pbk.)
    1. Venus (Planet)—Juvenile literature. [1. Venus (Planet)] I. Moser, Diane, 1944–
II. Title.III. Series.
QB621 .S65 2001
523.42—dc21

J
523.42
SPA

00-035902

Contents

Venus and the Moon (right) are reflected in a lake at dawn.

Chapter One

Venus, Earth's Sister

People have been watching Venus since ancient times. They couldn't miss it— Venus is brighter than anything else in the nighttime sky, except the Moon. Ancient astronomers thought Venus was two separate objects. One named "Morning Star" appeared in the east and another named "Evening Star" appeared in the west. Of course, we now know that Venus is one object, a planet, revolving around the Sun.

Each planet in our solar system is named after a character from Roman mythology. Venus was named after the Roman goddess of love and beauty—probably because it shines so brightly.

The History of Venus

About 4.6 billion years ago, our solar system started out as a cloud of gases called the **solar nebula.** A star, our Sun, formed at the center and the leftover material around it began to clump together, forming larger masses of material. Eventually, this material became what we now know as planets, moons, **asteroids**, **comets**, and **meteoroids**.

Our solar system began as a cloud of bright gases like this one.

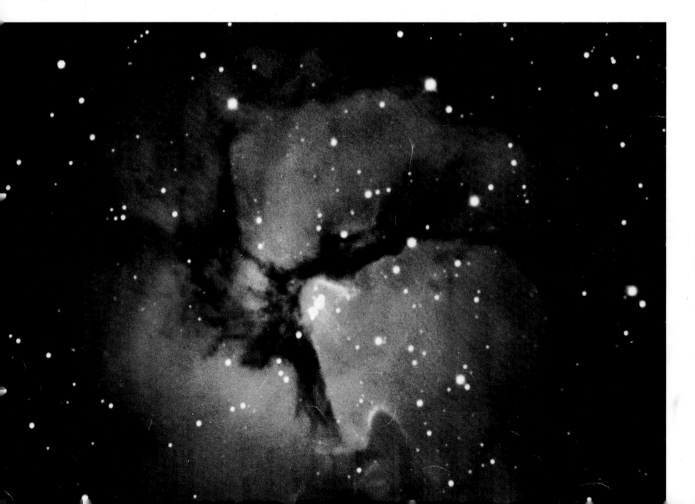

In our solar system, nine planets **revolve** around the Sun. The planets closest to the Sun are Mercury, Venus, Earth, and Mars. They are known as the terrestrial planets and are made up mostly of rock and metal. They have very few objects in orbit around them. Venus, the "second rock from the Sun," has no moon and orbits the Sun in an almost perfect circle.

A day on Venus is 243 times longer than a day on Earth. In fact, Venus's day is longer than its year. This is because Venus turns, or **rotates**, very slowly—much slower than Earth. Like other planets, Venus rotates on its **axis**, an imaginary line through its north and south poles. When a planet makes one full turn on its axis, it has completed one day. While Earth takes 24 hours to complete one rotation, Venus takes 5,832 hours. If you lived on Venus, you would spend about 1,458 hours in school each day! Also, Venus rotates in the opposite direction of Earth, so the Sun rises in the west and sets in the east.

Our Sister Planet

Despite these differences, some observations of Venus have led people to believe that Venus is "Earth's twin." Venus is about the same size as Earth. It is 7,520 miles (12,104 kilometers) across, while Earth is 7,927 miles (12,756 km) across. Venus's orbit brings it closer to Earth than any other planet's— only about 26 million miles (41.8 million km). Venus and Earth are both rocky planets composed of a similar type of volcanic rock. Exploration of Venus's surface has revealed

Moonlessness

Only two planets in the solar system have no moon. One is Venus; the other is Mercury.

This image of Venus has been colored to show the cloud structure.

mountains, valleys, and plains. And, like Earth, Venus has a thick, cloud-filled **atmosphere**—a mass of gases that surrounds the planet.

8

Comparing Venus and Earth

	Venus	Earth
Distance from Sun	67 million miles (108 million km)	93 million miles (150 million km)
One orbit around the Sun	225 Earth-days	365.25 Earth-days
One complete turn on its axis	243 Earth-days	1 Earth-day
Diameter	7,520 miles (12,104 km)	7,927 miles (12,756 km)
Composition of atmosphere	96.5 percent carbon dioxide, 3.5 percent nitrogen	78 percent nitrogen, 21 percent oxygen, 1 percent water

At one time, this thick atmosphere acted like a veil that hid the surface of Venus. Before humans were able to explore Venus's surface, many scientists and science-fiction writers thought the planet was moist and warm. Some even believed it might be covered with swamps. A few people thought giant creatures might live there, much as dinosaurs once lived in the forests and swamps of Earth. Other people wondered whether the thick clouds hid vast oceans and green countryside. A few imagined there might be cities there, built by an intelligent civilization. No one could see through the thick clouds of Venus, so anything seemed possible. The idea that Earth could have a sister planet inspired scientists to take a closer look at this mysterious, veiled world.

9

Deadly Heat and Acid Rain

We have since learned that there's a lot about Venus that's very different from Earth. For example, Venus is unbearably hot. If you walked on the surface of Venus, you would barbecue your feet! In fact, your entire body would broil in the intense heat. The temperature sometimes climbs as high as 882 degrees Fahrenheit (472 degrees Celsius). On Earth, about 71 percent of the surface is covered with water. Our clouds are made of suspended droplets of water. Venus has no water—no oceans or rivers or streams. The clouds on Venus are made of tiny drops of sulfuric acid—the stuff you find in car batteries. Venus is closer to the Sun's fiery furnace, so when it rains on Venus the acid that drops from the clouds boils away before it reaches the ground! Humans would not be able to breathe on Venus either. Even though "Earth's twin" has an atmosphere, it is composed mostly of carbon dioxide. Humans would choke to death almost instantly.

Clearly, Venus would be a very unpleasant place to visit. But, scientists like to study Venus because it is so similar to

Earth, and yet so different. They want to know if Earth could someday become like Venus. They would like to discover why Earth became such a good place to live, and how we can make sure our environment never gets to be like Venus's.

Volcanoes and lava flows have helped make Venus a very hot place, as this artwork shows.

From Earth, Venus
shows phases, like
the Moon.

Chapter Two

A Closer View

Early astronomers studied the motions of Venus and the other planets, but they couldn't see much else with the naked eye. Then in 1609, the Italian scientist Galileo Galilei first used a telescope to look at the nighttime skies. When he did, Galileo noticed a striking fact—Venus, like the Moon, appears to change shape and size to viewers on Earth. Over time, telescopes improved and scientists like Russia's Mikhail Lomonosov developed creative ways of gathering information about Venus. This closer view of Venus led to some surprising discoveries.

Phases of Venus

From Earth you can see the phases of the Moon without a telescope. In the night sky, we can see the Moon because light from the Sun reflects off its surface. As the Moon revolves around Earth, the Sun lights up different sections. The Moon seems to change shape because we see only the parts that are lit by the Sun. The different shapes we see are called phases and include a crescent, half-moon, and full moon. During a full moon, the whole disk of the Moon is lit up. By studying these phases, we can follow the path of the Moon as it moves around Earth.

With pen and paper, Galileo sketched the phases of the Moon. When he looked at Venus, he discovered phases there too. He studied the pattern of light as it hit Venus and realized that Venus must be located between Earth and the Sun, and that both planets must be orbiting the Sun.

This idea of a **heliocentric**, or Sun-centered, universe had been published in 1543 by a Polish astronomer named Nicolaus Copernicus. Many people rejected this idea, however, including the powerful Roman Catholic Church. They supported the theory developed by Ptolemy in about A.D. 150. Ptolemy believed in a **geocentric**, or Earth-centered, universe in which the Sun and all the planets revolve around Earth. Based partly on his observations of Venus, Galileo rejected Ptolemy's theory and became convinced that Copernicus's theory was correct. He realized that the Sun, not Earth, must be at the center of the solar system.

Stubborn Scientist

Galileo talked to everyone he knew about the Sun-centered solar system. But, since the Roman Catholic Church still supported the belief that the planets and the Sun revolved around Earth, Galileo was soon in trouble with Church authorities. They put him on trial and sentenced him to life imprisonment. He was put under house arrest until he died in 1642. Finally, in November 1992—350 years later—Pope John Paul II acknowledged that the Catholic Church had wrongly condemned Galileo's work.

The Veiled Planet

Even with Galileo's telescope, Venus, along with most of the other planets in the solar system, remained a mystery. By the following century, though, telescopes had become more powerful, and astronomers had learned some new tricks. In 1761

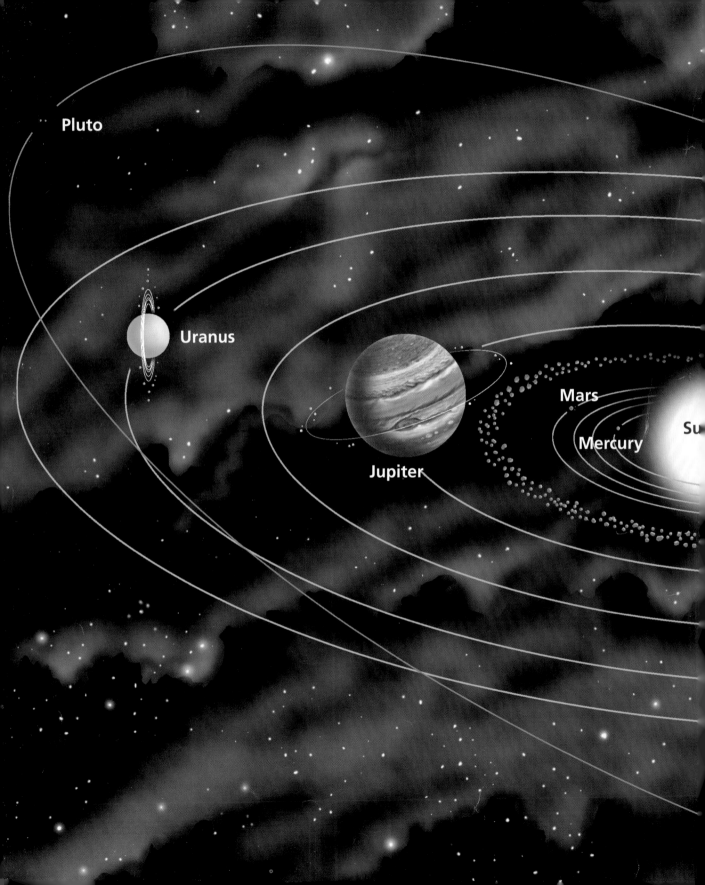

The Solar System

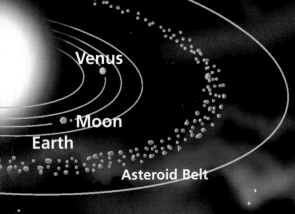

Venus

Moon

Earth

Asteroid Belt

Saturn

Neptune

Russian scientist Mikhail Lomonosov was observing Venus closely to try to obtain new measurements. He then discovered that the veil covering Venus was actually a thick atmosphere.

Lomonosov had planned to get a measurement of the diameter of Venus that would be more accurate than anything obtained so far. He timed his observation to catch Venus as it crossed, or was in **transit** across, the disk of the Sun. The planet would then be clearly outlined as a dark shadow in the Sun's bright light, and a more precise measurement would be possible.

Mikhail Lomonosov (1711–1765) discovered that Venus had an atmosphere.

Russian "Renaissance Man"

At the age of 17, Mikhail Lomonosov left home and ran off to Moscow, where he hoped to get an education. At that time, people of noble birth were given preference in schools, so Lomonosov told authorities that he was of noble descent. School officials probably didn't believe him, but, after seeing what Lomonosov had learned on his own, they gave him a chance at the schooling he wanted. He soon qualified for entry to the University of Petersburg where he studied science. Later, he moved on to advanced work in chemistry at the University of Marburg in Germany. He became a professor of chemistry at the University of Petersburg in 1745, but he was also known for his poetry and his discoveries in chemistry, physics, and astronomy.

Lomonosov was in for a big surprise. When the disk of Venus was fully surrounded by the light of the Sun, the edge was still not sharp and clear as he had expected. Instead, it was fuzzy and blurry. At first Lomonosov couldn't imagine why. Then he thought about it. If Venus had an atmosphere, a viewer on Earth would not see the hard-edged surface outlined against the Sun. Instead, the viewer would see the fuzzy edges of the clouds or gases that make up Venus's atmosphere. Lomonosov had discovered an atmosphere on another planet!

By the 1950s, new telescope techniques helped scientists learn more about the atmosphere of Venus, but still no one could see beyond the thick pea-soup fog that surrounded the planet.

Robot spacecraft like this one have helped us take a closer look at Venus.

Chapter Three

Robots Visit Venus

By the early 1960s, scientists in two nations had developed more effective ways to explore the planets of the solar system—robot spacecraft. Instead of going into space themselves, scientists could send these robots, or "probes," to take a closer look and send back information electronically. The two nations were the United States and the former Union of Soviet Socialist Republics, also known as the Soviet Union. This vast country was composed of today's Russia, Ukraine, and several smaller countries. The "space race" between these two nations provided us with valuable information about the surface and atmosphere of Venus.

Flying Robots

The Space Age began with the launch of the first satellite by the Soviet Union. In October 1957, *Sputnik 1* was placed in orbit around Earth. The U.S. satellite *Explorer 1* followed in January 1958. By 1959, the Soviet Union had sent the first spacecraft beyond Earth's orbit—to the Moon, the only object in space that is closer to Earth than Venus.

Could spacecraft from Earth also reach the closest planet? Both countries geared up for the challenge. Venus was the first goal because it was closest, but getting there wasn't easy. Many spacecraft never made their way beyond Earth's orbit. Launches failed. Engines fizzled. Radios failed to transmit.

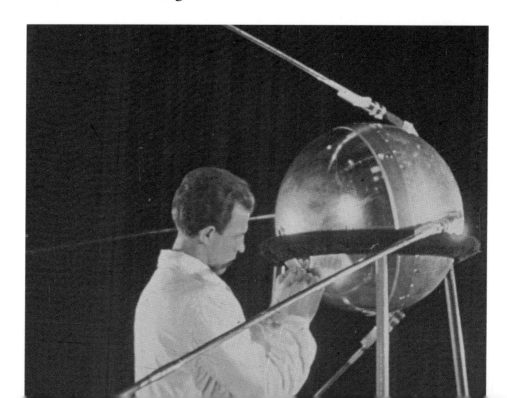

A scientist inspects Sputnik 1.

Finally, on December 14, 1962, *Mariner 2* whizzed by Venus. With its toolbox full of instruments, the American spacecraft weighed 446 pounds (202 kilograms). *Mariner 2* sent back information about the solar wind, magnetic fields between planets, and many other interesting features of the solar system. But the big news was that Earthlings at last had their first close-up view of Venus.

Mariner 2 came within 22,000 miles (35,406 km) of Venus. As it sped by, the little spacecraft sent 42 minutes of reports to the Jet Propulsion Laboratory (JPL) in Pasadena, California. The news was surprising. Scientists were amazed at the intense heat on the planet's surface. At more than four times the boiling point of water, it was hotter than anyone had ever imagined! Little or no protective magnetic field appeared to surround Venus. Also, the atmosphere was composed mostly of carbon dioxide and had almost no oxygen. These were the first signs that life as we know it could not possibly grow or even survive on Venus. Visions of steamy jungles and roaming dinosaurs disappeared in December 1962.

Mariner 2 was the first spacecraft to visit another planet. This full-scale model hangs from the ceiling at the National Air and Space Museum.

Taking a Deeper Look

The Soviets wanted to find out what Venus's surface looked like. They set to work creating a spacecraft that would be able to land on Venus. To do this, the spacecraft would have to be tough enough to withstand the pressure of Venus's heavy atmosphere. Finally, in 1970, they succeeded. On December 15, *Venera 7* landed on Venus and sent information to Earth for 23 minutes. Scientists were excited. Not only was this the first report on the mysterious surface beneath the clouds of Venus, it was the first report ever from the surface of another planet.

Five years later, two Soviet landers named *Venera 9* and *Venera 10* relayed television images of the first "worm's-eye view" of the planet. One spacecraft landed amid chunks of

Scientists assemble the Soviet spacecraft Venera 9.

broken rock. The other sent back views of flat slabs of dusty rock. From the landers' instruments, scientists learned the rocks were similar to rocks formed around volcanoes on Earth.

Fly-by Weather Reports

While the Soviet Union explored the surface, the United States found new ways to study Venus's atmosphere. *Mariner 10* lifted off on a night launch from Florida on November 4, 1973 on its way to Mercury. Engineers at the National Aeronautics and Space Administration (NASA) had planned

Mariner 10 *used a "gravity assist" from Venus to increase speed on its way to Mercury.*

the route so that *Mariner 10* would get a **gravity assist** from Venus. Scientists predicted that as *Mariner 10* looped around Venus, the planet's force of gravity would act like a slingshot and propel the spacecraft toward Mercury. This plan would help *Mariner 10* reach its destination faster and it would allow the spacecraft to collect more information about Venus's atmosphere as it flew by.

It took 93 days for the spacecraft to arrive within 3,585 miles (5,770 km) of Venus. Above the clouds that hung over Venus's sizzling surface, *Mariner 10* began taking pictures. But these were not just ordinary pictures. Unlike regular photographs, these images were able to show movement and detailed layers in the clouds.

Mariner 10 sent more than 4,000 images back to Earth. From these images, scientists discovered that the upper atmosphere of Venus moves with incredible speed—much faster than the planet itself. The cloud tops of Venus rotate at a superfast speed of 205 miles (330 km) per hour, while the surface atmosphere almost stands still. Scientists also learned that Venus's upper atmosphere absorbs most of the Sun's heat. This means that the planet's atmosphere is actually hotter than its surface.

When *Mariner 10* went on to visit Mercury, it became the first spacecraft to visit more than one planet. Three more spacecraft visited Venus on the way to other destinations. Two were Soviet missions and the third was launched by the United States.

Cloudy View

More spacecraft have studied the atmosphere of Venus than any other atmosphere in the solar system, except Earth's.

The Soviet Union's *Vega 1* and *Vega 2* whizzed by in 1985. They released four probes as they sped by Venus toward a rendezvous with Halley's Comet. Two of the probes were landers that took a close look at the soil of Venus. They also released two atmospheric weather balloons that reported measurements from 31 to 34 miles (50 to 55 km) above the surface.

A Vega *spacecraft is pictured here during its assembly in the Soviet Union.*

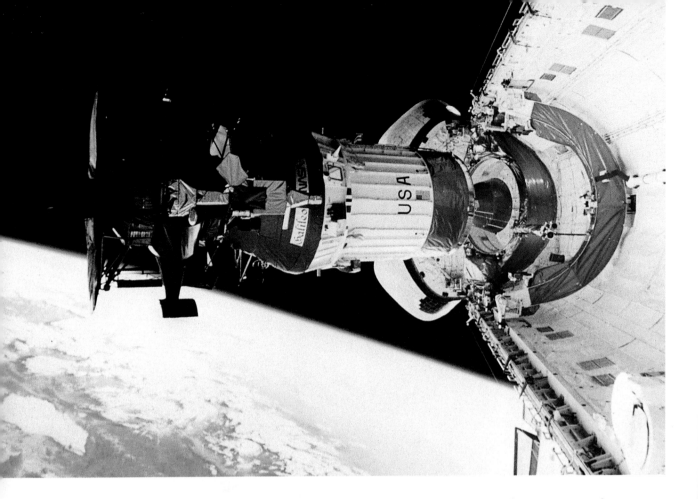

Galileo is released from the space shuttle Atlantis.

The U.S. launched *Galileo* in 1989. The spacecraft was on its way to Jupiter and would travel beyond the **asteroid belt**, a region between Mars and Jupiter where most asteroids orbit. But first, *Galileo* would fly by Venus for a gravity assist. The spacecraft carried a special instrument called a near-infrared mapping spectrometer (NIMS). NIMS could take images at near-infrared wavelengths, so scientists thought it would be a great idea to focus NIMS on Venus as it whizzed by. As *Galileo* traveled past Venus, scientists got ready to turn on NIMS. However, NIMS had somehow heated up—and was too hot to use. Scientists tried to cool it down, but time was ticking away.

Soon Venus would no longer be in view. Finally, just in time, NIMS cooled off and the engineers opened the instrument.

NIMS captured unique images of the part of Venus facing away from the Sun. Regular optical photographs would have been completely black, but the infrared images taken by NIMS showed heat radiation leaking through the dark atmosphere. These images also showed cloud structures deep within the atmosphere. After its stunning success at Venus, *Galileo* carried NIMS on to other encounters.

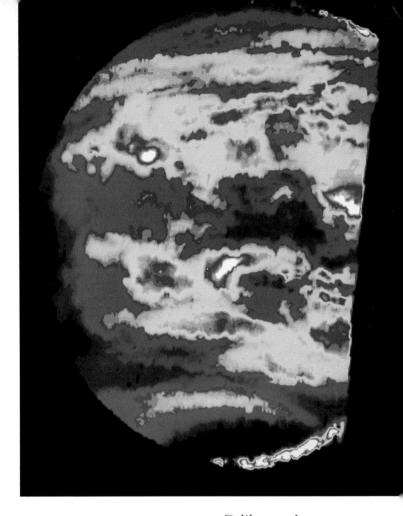

Galileo used near-infrared wavelengths to take this false-color image of the nightside of Venus.

Pioneer Journeys

From *Mariner 10*, scientists had gained new views of the clouds and the weather systems of Venus, and some of the Venera landers had taken a few images at ground level. *Galileo* would give them a different view of the clouds. However, none of these missions let scientists see through the thick veil of clouds to find out what Venus was really like. In 1978, the United States launched a new type of spacecraft in an effort to break through Venus's atmosphere and discover more about the surface. NASA had developed a series of spacecraft called *Pioneers*. This name would remind people of the pioneers who traveled in covered wagons into the unknown territory of the western United States. It was a good name for a series of explorer spacecraft. Two of them headed for Venus in 1978—one in May and one in August.

Pioneer Venus 1 collected information about Venus's surface using **radar**. Radar is a system that sends out radio waves. The waves bounce off distant objects and are measured when they return. Scientists used the measurements from *Pioneer Venus 1*

This radar map was created from information gathered by Pioneer Venus 1.

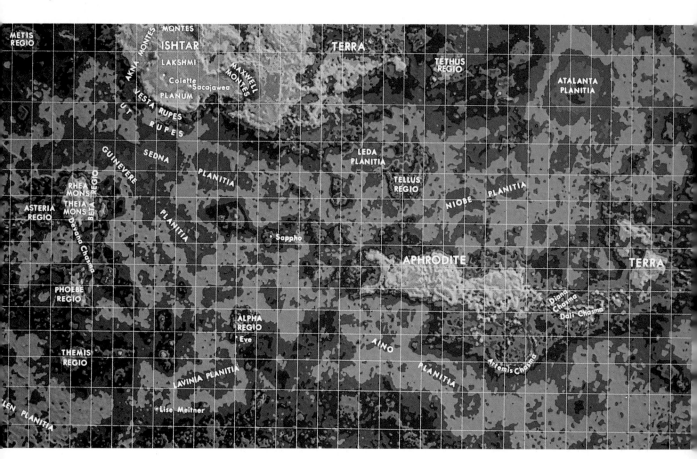

to create maps showing the **topography**, or surface profile of the planet. At last, a picture of the landforms of Venus began to take shape.

What scientists saw surprised them. Venus had continents—raised landmasses as large as Australia and Africa. Where Earth has oceans around its continents, though, Venus had only hot, dry plains. Scientists named the smaller continent Aphrodite Terra and the larger continent Ishtar Terra.

The images revealed mountains, volcanoes, plains, plateaus, valleys, and many craters formed by the impact of **meteorites**. Radar studies conducted on Earth had suggested some of these formations, but now scientists could actually see their width and height. *Pioneer Venus 1* provided the first detailed view of 90 percent of Venus's surface. Scientists could see that the landscape greatly resembled Earth's, and they began to think harder about why Venus was so different from Earth in other ways.

Meanwhile, *Pioneer Venus 2* (also known as the *Pioneer Venus* Multiprobe) set out on a different mission in August 1978. A spacecraft called a bus carried one large probe and three smaller probes that would each test a different area of Venus. The three smaller probes had names: the night probe, the day probe, and the North probe. These robots gathered information about the temperature, circulation, composition, and pressure of Venus's atmosphere. The large probe and the night probe were released on the side of Venus that faced away from the Sun, called the night side. The North probe and the day

It Keeps Going and Going...

Pioneer Venus 1 was launched on May 20, 1978, and began orbiting Venus on December 4, 1978. It completed its mission in 1979, but kept mapping and reporting for another 13 years. NASA lost radio contact with this spacecraft on October 8, 1992.

probe were released on the side of Venus that faced the Sun, called the day side. The North probe was released farther north than the day probe. As expected, NASA scientists lost contact with three of the probes when they hit the surface. The day probe was the only probe that sent signals after landing. NASA lost contact with the bus that carried the probes while it was still passing through the atmosphere.

Mapping Venus

In the 1980s, Russia continued to launch *Venera* spacecraft. *Venera 13* and *14* were launched in 1981, and each carried two parts—a flyby and a lander. The flyby split off to observe the planet from above as it whizzed by. The lander continued its journey to Venus's surface, where it landed and reported what it saw. The spacecraft sent back color and black-and-white images of the surface, tested rocks, drilled down below the crust, and scooped up and tested soil samples. Two more spacecraft were launched in 1983—*Venera 15* and *16*. They

One of the first color pictures of the surface of Venus, taken by Venera 13.

were called "orbiters" because they orbited Venus as they gathered information. Like *Pioneer Venus 1*, these two spacecraft used radar to measure the surface. But the measurements gathered by *Venera 15* and *16* were much more detailed and allowed scientists to determine the height of volcanoes and the depth of craters in Venus's northern hemisphere.

Scientists were soon ready to take the next step in exploring Venus's surface. The spacecraft *Magellan* was named for Ferdinand Magellan, the great explorer who was the first to travel around the world and prove that it was round. *Magellan* lived up to its name. When it left the shuttle bay of *Atlantis* in

Magellan *is launched from the Space Shuttle* Atlantis *and begins its voyage to Venus.*

May 1989, it became the first interplanetary spacecraft launched from a space shuttle.

The spacecraft *Magellan* orbited Venus for four years and imaged 98 percent of its surface. The images showed details as small as 240 feet (73 meters) across—smaller than a football field. As the data began coming in, the NASA scientists were able to see crisp, clear radar images. These images showed features never seen before on another planet and proved we had much to learn from our nearest neighbor.

An Astronaut Looks at Earth

Mary Cleave was one of the astronauts on the space shuttle *Atlantis* who launched *Magellan*. She does more than launch satellites though. Most astronauts specialize in one area of study. Cleave is an ecologist, a scientist who looks at the way living things interact with one another and with Earth's environment. During two flights aboard *Atlantis*, Cleave observed changes on Earth's surface. She is concerned that human activity is changing Earth too rapidly and hopes to learn more about Venus and what happened to make it so unfriendly to life.

Major Missions to Venus

Spacecraft	Year of Arrival	Type of Mission	Mission Highlights
Mariner 2	1962	Flyby	First successful mission to another planet
Venera 7	1970	Lander	First report from the surface of the planet
Mariner 10	1974	Orbiter	First close-up ultraviolet images of cloud tops
Venera 9 and 10	1975	Orbiter/landers	First photos from the surface
Pioneer Venus 1	1978	Orbiter	Radar mapping, first global view
Pioneer Venus 2	1978	Multiprobe	Five probes of the atmosphere
Venera 13 and 14	1982	Flyby/landers	First color pictures of the surface
Venera 15 and 16	1983	Orbiters	High-resolution radar mapping of surface
Vega 1 and 2	1985	Flyby, dropping 2 landers and 2 atmospheric balloons	Dropped off landers and balloons on their way to Halley's comet
Galileo	1990	Flyby	Took infrared images of the planet's night side
Magellan	1990	Orbiter	Captured highly detailed radar maps of 98 percent of the surface

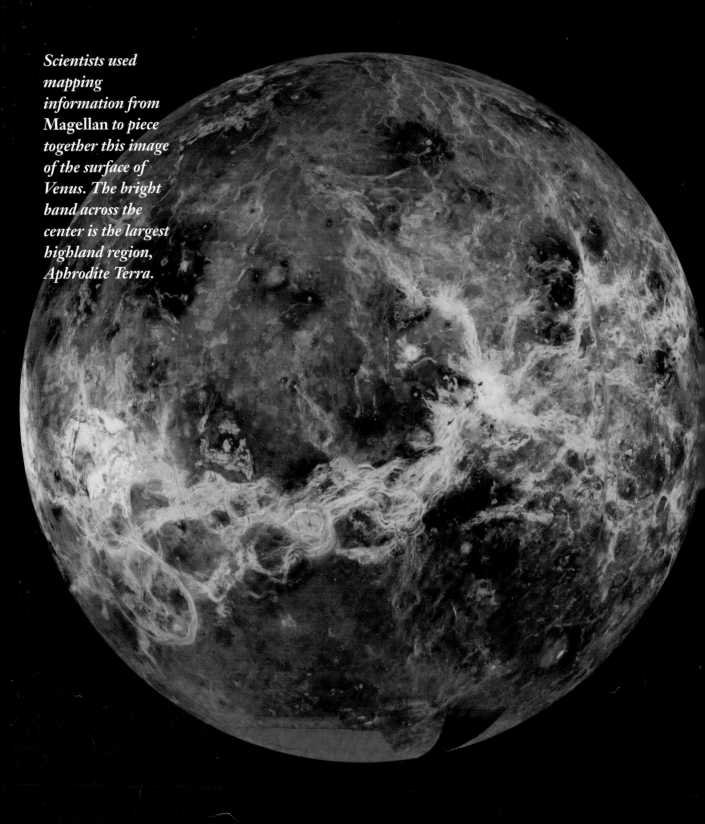

Scientists used mapping information from Magellan to piece together this image of the surface of Venus. The bright band across the center is the largest highland region, Aphrodite Terra.

Chapter Four

World of Weird Shapes

Most of what we now know about Venus's surface came from the radar images taken by *Magellan*. The detailed maps created from these images finally provided an overview of the planet, from the ground up. Scientists learn a lot by comparing these maps to what they know about Earth's surface.

For example, the formation of mountains is different on the two planets. Continent-sized slabs beneath Earth's surface, called tectonic plates, shift and press against one another. When the edges of these plates come together, they sometimes push up and form mountain ranges and volcanoes. In other parts of the world, the plates move apart and create rift valleys. Venus has mountains and volcanoes, but scientists cannot find any evidence that the surface of Venus has been affected by moving plates below the surface. Scientists think many of the formations on Venus were caused by volcanic activity.

Magellan sent back images of massive volcanic peaks. Some of them are as high as 35,000 feet (10,668 m) above the plains. That's higher than Mount Everest, Earth's highest peak. When the Soviet Union's surface landers tested the soil on Venus, they found evidence of volcanic lava rocks in several locations.

The remnants of volcanoes on Venus have created some unique shapes that are not found on other planets. In some areas, unusual formations called "ticks" formed when parts of a volcano's sides caved in, leaving ridged marks that look like legs extending from the rounded cone. From *Magellan*, the formation looked like a giant wood tick. Other volcanoes have lava flows that look like bright petals extending into the area around the cone. These are

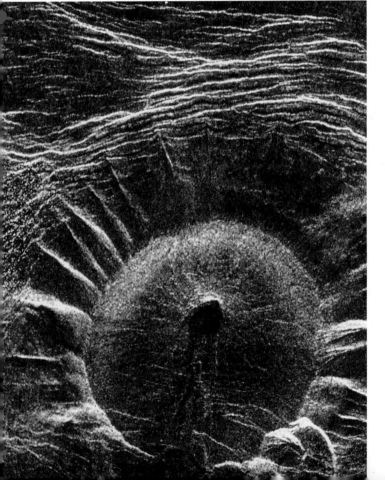

Magellan discovered volcanoes with leg-like features that make them look like huge ticks. These features formed when the sides of the volcanoes caved in.

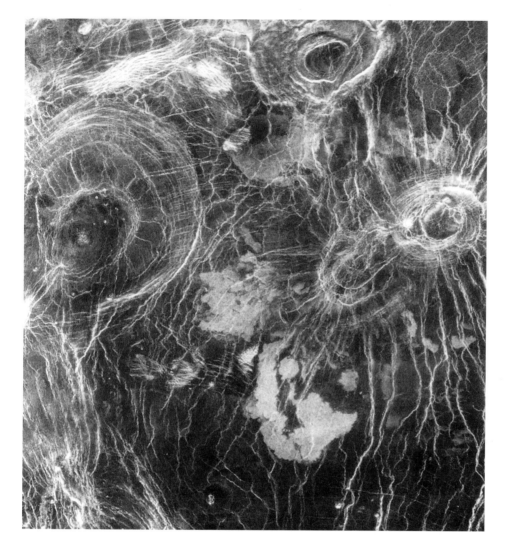

These volcanoes on Venus have spidery, web-like features called arachnoids.

called "anemonae" (the plural of anemone), after the sea animals on Earth that look like flowers. Still other volcanic domes show spidery arms stretching out from the center. They look like cobwebs, which earned them the name "arachnoids," meaning spider-like structures.

Magellan gave us a closer look at the strange features called coronae, first noticed by Russian scientists in the 1980s. These circular fractures look like bulls-eyes and measure 124 to 1,243 miles (200 to 2,000 km) across. The largest corona, named Artemis after the Greek goddess of wild animals and hunting, is 1,300 miles (2,100 km) across and 3.8 miles (6 km) deep. Scientists think these structures formed when molten lava below the surface bulged up and cracked the crust. Then small amounts of lava flowed out and the center sagged, forming a valley.

Scientists think that Venus's "pancake" volcano domes are formed when oozing lava is flattened by gravitational force.

Perhaps the strangest of *Magellan's* discoveries was a type of structure found nowhere else in the solar system. Huge, flattened domes that look like groups of giant pancakes 15 miles (24 km) across rise up as much as 2,000 feet (610 m) from the

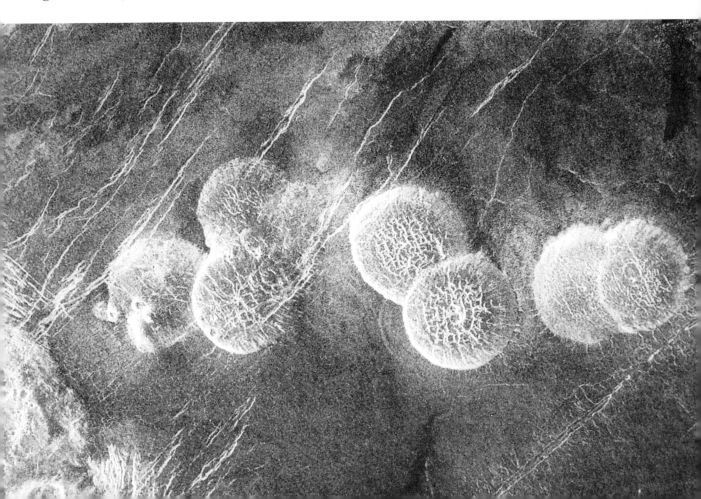

surface of Venus. Scientists think these "pancake domes" were formed by slowly oozing lava so stiff that it piled up high. Then **gravity**, the force that pulls objects toward the center of the planet, flattened it out on top.

Repaved Surface

Scientists often try to estimate the age of an object in the solar system by studying the number of craters on its surface. On Venus, however, studying the craters tells us more about Venus's atmosphere and volcanic activity than it does about the planet's age.

No crater on Venus is smaller than about 1.3 miles (2 km) across. Scientists have figured out that smaller craters never form because smaller objects are blocked by the planet's thick, hot, high-pressure atmosphere. They are crushed to powder long before they could plow into the surface and leave their mark. Objects with no atmosphere, such as the Moon, are covered with thousands of craters of all sizes.

Scientists now think that, within Venus, the **mantle** swells from time to time with hot, upward-flowing currents called **mantle plumes**. These plumes erupt through the surface to form a volcano. Crustal rocks on Venus are always just below the melting point because the surface of Venus is so hot. When a mantle plume nears the surface, the rocks of the crust become hot enough to melt and ooze, and the lava pours out. Scientists think this may explain why the surface of Venus is covered with lava.

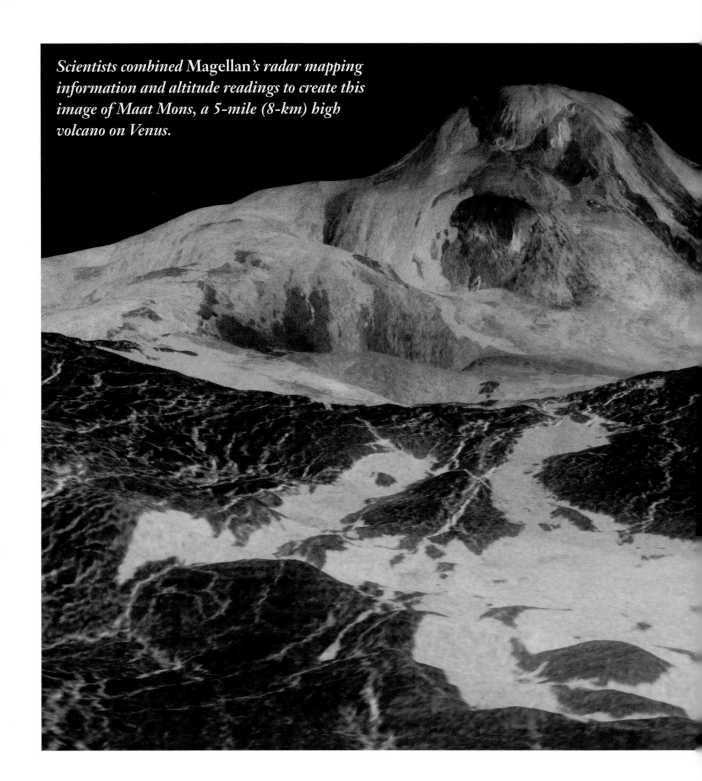

Scientists combined Magellan's radar mapping information and altitude readings to create this image of Maat Mons, a 5-mile (8-km) high volcano on Venus.

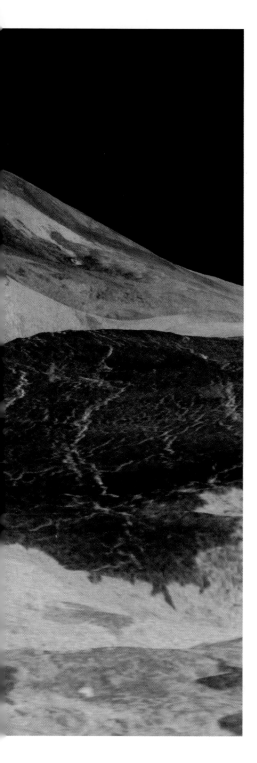

Whenever volcanoes spew lava, and bulges of **magma** ooze through the crust, the surface of Venus tends to lose the signs of its history. Lava smooths out the surface. It fills ancient craters and gashes left by billions of years of colliding meteorites. Scientists call this process "repaving the surface." The oldest surface feature on Venus is 800 million years old. Scientists believe that volcanic activity caused lava to flow over the surface and fill in any craters formed before this time.

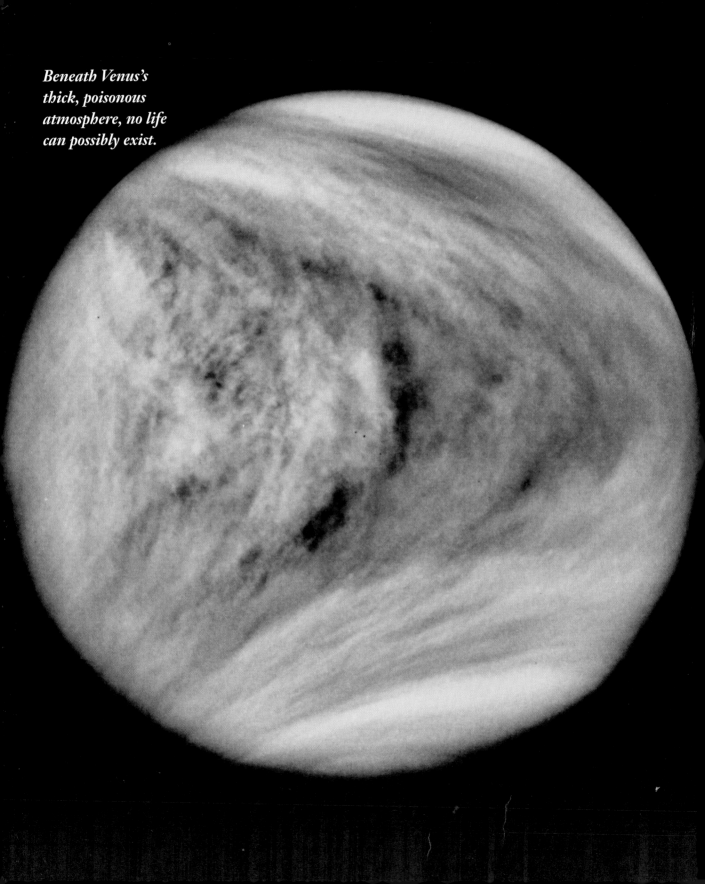

Beneath Venus's thick, poisonous atmosphere, no life can possibly exist.

Chapter Five

Lifeless Greenhouse

As scientists studied Venus, they recognized how closely the planet's surface and its atmosphere are linked. Together, the surface and atmosphere have played key roles in Venus's history and account for the similarities and differences between Earth and Venus. By comparing Earth and Venus, scientists hope to learn how to take better care of Earth's environment.

We know that both planets heat up deep inside. Magma pushes up through weak spots in the crust, forming volcanoes, and the volcanoes release carbon dioxide into the atmosphere. But the atmosphere of each planet is quite different. On Earth, the atmosphere is composed mostly of nitrogen and oxygen. On Venus, the atmosphere is mainly carbon dioxide. By looking at the surfaces of both planets, we can begin to understand these differences.

On Earth, the carbon dioxide from volcanoes quickly becomes dissolved in the waters of streams, rivers, lakes, and oceans. Plant life combines carbon dioxide and water with energy from sunlight to form sugars and starches in a process

On Earth, the atmosphere supports a widely diverse population of living things, including 6 billion humans.

called **photosynthesis**. Tiny microscopic animals combine carbon dioxide with calcium to make their shells. Together, these processes remove large quantities of carbon dioxide from our atmosphere.

The surface and atmosphere of Venus tell quite a different story. Venus has no water to absorb the carbon dioxide released from the volcanoes. The probes from *Pioneer Venus 2* discovered that the atmosphere of Venus has a tiny bit of water vapor. They also found a very small amount of free oxygen— oxygen that is not combined with something else to form a substance such as sulfuric acid or water. Scientists think the presence of these tiny amounts of oxygen may mean that Venus had surface water long ago when the planet formed. But heat from the Sun caused the water to boil away and no ocean existed to dissolve the carbon dioxide.

So, with nowhere else to go, the carbon dioxide hangs in a thick blanket over Venus's surface. Because of this, the atmosphere on Venus is ninety times heavier than the atmosphere on Earth. From the photos sent by *Venera 9* and *10* and *Venera 13* and *14*, **planetologists** learned what the view is like underneath this blanket—at ground level. It is clear—not foggy as everyone had long imagined. The view is much like an overcast day on Earth—bright light diffused through yellow clouds. As we found out from the robot spacecraft that explored the atmosphere, the clouds are made of sulfuric acid—a powerful, toxic substance that can eat right through the hardest metals.

Sizzling Raindrops

In 1978, *Pioneer Venus* probes found acid rain pelting down from a height of 19 to 24 miles (31 to 39 km). But, unlike rain on Earth, this raining acid never reaches the surface. As it nears the surface, the searing heat boils it away.

Venus's Greenhouse

The blanket of carbon dioxide in the atmosphere creates Venus's extreme heat. Like the glass windows of a greenhouse, the heavy layer of atmosphere lets the Sun's radiation pass inside, and then locks it in. Infrared radiation is trapped, blocked from leaving the planet's surface. Scientists call this the **greenhouse effect**.

Some experts believe that if Earth had formed 83 million miles (134 million km) from the Sun instead of 93 million miles (150 million km), our planet would have been much hotter. The Sun's heat would be more intense because it would reach Earth faster. As a result, oceans would have boiled away,

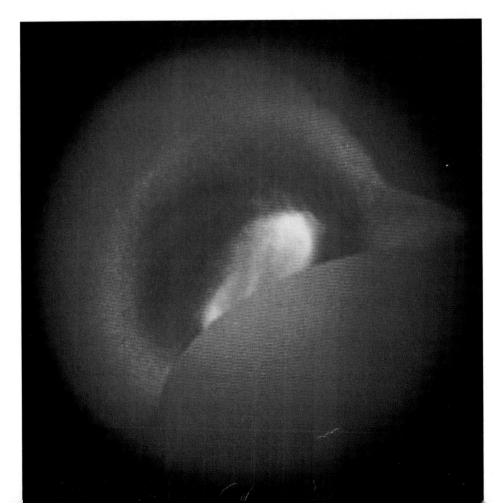

This infrared photo taken by Pioneer Venus *shows the clouds over the north pole of* Venus.

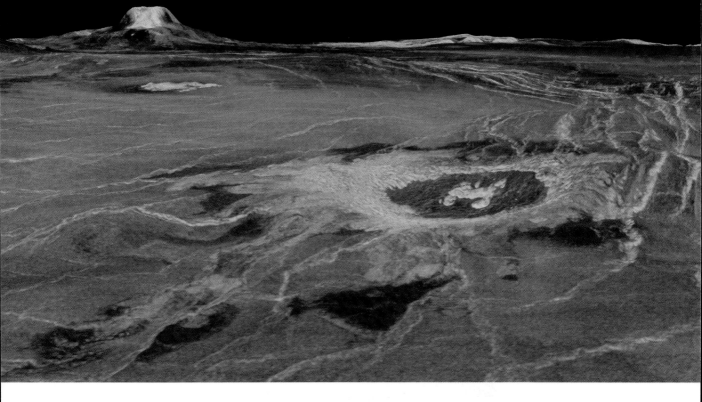

producing more water vapor and carbon dioxide in the air. This buildup of water vapor and carbon dioxide would trap even more heat. Warming would increase, and Earth—like Venus—would have an extreme greenhouse effect.

Could Earth someday be as barren of living things as the searing hot surface of Venus?

In this scenario, changing Earth's position in relation to the Sun would change its climate completely. Since such small changes can make a very big difference in climate and environment, it's important to closely monitor human activities. Although we do not have the ability to change the position of Earth in the solar system, we can cause our climate to change.

Factory pollution increases the amount of carbon dioxide in our atmosphere, which can trap heat and lead to an increase in global temperatures.

We know we have already increased carbon dioxide in Earth's atmosphere. Our automobiles and factories release huge quantities of carbon dioxide into the air. Acid rain has fallen in areas where industries emit large amounts of pollutants into the air. If we are not careful, our planet could become as unlivable as our mysterious neighbor.

So Similar, yet so Different

Today, scientists know much more about Venus than the ancient astronomers knew. Yet the planet remains intriguing and mysterious. Its size is so similar to Earth's, it has a thick atmosphere that looks much like Earth's, and in many other ways it resembles Earth. Yet, in some ways it is amazingly different. Scientists believe that the evolution of life on Earth caused a big change in our planet's atmosphere—an important key to our planet's history. Would the evolution of heat-resistant life forms on Venus have caused the planet's history to unfold differently? As scientists continue to examine Earth, Venus, and other planets, we hope to find out more and more about how things work on planets, in solar systems, and in the universe. One day, we will also understand more about the unfolding mysteries of Earth's mysterious "twin."

Glossary

asteroid—a large piece of rock that formed at the same time as the Sun and planets.

asteroid belt—the region in space between Mars and Jupiter where most asteroids are found. It is 100 million miles (161 million km) wide.

atmosphere—the gases that surround a planet or other body in space.

axis—the imaginary line running from pole to pole through a planet's center. A planet spins, or rotates, along its axis.

comet—a small ball of rock and ice that orbits the Sun. When it approaches the Sun, some of the ice melts and releases gases. These gases form a tail behind each comet.

geocentric—having Earth as the center.

gravity—the force that pulls objects toward the center of a planet or other body in space.

gravity assist—using a planet's force of gravity during flyby to help propel a spacecraft toward its destination at a faster speed.

greenhouse effect—heating influence of an atmosphere that heats the surface higher than it otherwise would be; the greenhouse effect on Venus is extreme.

heliocentric—having the Sun as the center.

magma—molten matter beneath the planet's crust.

mantle—a geologically different region below the crust of a planet, located between the crust and the core.

mantle plumes—hot, upward flowing currents of magma or molten rock within the mantle.

meteorite—a particle of dust or rock from space that hits the surface of another object, such as a moon or planet.

meteoroid—a rocky or metallic object of relatively small size, usually once part of a comet or asteroid.

photosynthesis—a process in which plant life combines carbon dioxide and water with energy from sunlight to form sugars and starches.

planetologists—scientists who study planets.

radar—a system that bounces radio waves off a distant object and measures the returning waves in order to locate that object.

revolve—to move in a path, or orbit, around another object. Earth revolves around the Sun, making a complete trip in one year.

rotate—to turn or spin around a central point.

solar nebula—the giant cloud of gases and dust from which the Sun and the planets were formed.

topography—the description or mapping of a planet's physical surface features.

transit—passage of a smaller body in front of a larger body (as Venus crossing in front of the Sun).

To Find Out More

Books

The news from space changes fast, so it's always a good idea to check the copyright date on books to make sure that you are reading current information.

Branley, Franklyn Mansfield. *Venus: Magellan Explores Our Twin Planet*. New York: HarperCollins Children's Books, 1994.

Brimner, Larry Dane. *Venus*. New York: Children's Press, 1998.

Campbell, Ann Jeanette. *The New York Public Library Amazing Space: A Book of Answers for Kids*. New York: John Wiley & Sons, 1997.

Dickinson, Terence. *Other Worlds: A Beginner's Guide to Planets and Moons*. Willowdale, Ontario: Firefly Books, 1995.

Gustafson, John. *Planets, Moons, & Meteors: The Young Stargazer's Guide to the Galaxy*. New York: Julian Messner, 1992.

Hartmann, William K. and Don Miller. *The Grand Tour*. New York: Workman Publishing, 1993.

Simon, Seymour. *Venus*. New York: Mulberry Paperback Books, 1998.

Vogt, Gregory L. *The Solar System Facts and Exploration*. Scientific American Sourcebooks. New York: Twenty-First Century Books, 1995.

_____, *Venus*. Brookfield, CT: Millbrook Press, 1996.

CD-ROMs

Beyond Planet Earth
For Macintosh and PC (DOS, Windows, OS2), from the Discovery Channel School Multimedia. An interactive journey to the planets, including Venus, with video from NASA and *Voyager* missions and more than 200 photographs. Discovery Channel School; P.O. Box 970; Oxon Hill, MD 20750-0970

Venus Explorer for IBM
Includes images of Venus's craters, channels, chasms, mountains, volcanic domes, calderas, and coronas. Uses data from *Magellan* spacecraft. For the IBM PC. Available from Andromeda Software, Inc.; P.O. Box 605-N; Amherst, NY 14226-0605

Organizations and Online Sites

The Astronomical Society of the Pacific
390 Ashton Avenue
San Francisco, CA 94112
http://www.aspsky.org

NASA Ask a Space Scientist
http://image.gsfc.nasa.gov/poetry/ask/askmag.html#list
Interactive page where NASA scientists answer your questions about astronomy, space, and space missions. Also has archives and Fact Sheets.

The Nine Planets: A Multimedia Tour of the Solar System
http://www.seds.org/nineplanets/nineplanets/nineplanets.html
Includes excellent material on Venus and other planets from the Students for the Exploration and Development of Space, University of Arizona.

Planetary Missions
http://nssdc.gsfc.nasa.gov/planetary/projects.html
Page of NASA links to all current and past missions, a one-stop shopping center to a wealth of information.

The Planetary Society
65 North Carolina Avenue
Pasadena, CA 91106-2301
http://www.planetary.org

Welcome to the Planets
http://pds.jpl.nasa.gov/planets/
Tour of the solar system with lots of pictures and information. Created by the California Institute of Technology for NASA/Jet Propulsion Laboratory.

Windows to the Universe
http://windows.ivv.nasa.gov/
NASA site, developed by the University of Michigan, includes sections on "Our Planet," "Our Solar System," "Space Missions," and "Kids' Space." Choose from presentation levels of beginner, intermediate, or advanced. To begin exploring, go to the URL above and choose "Enter the Site."

A Note on Sources

When we write about space science, we like to find the most up-to-date sources we can because scientists keep finding out more and more about the universe. We read as many of the latest books as we can find. (You should see our house—it has wall-to-wall books!) We find recent articles in science magazines such as *Scientific American* and *Science News*. We also use the Internet a lot. The National Aeronautics and Space Administration (NASA) keeps us up to date by e-mailing us the latest reports from scientists who study the data from spacecraft such as *Magellan*. We also check the NASA web pages (such as those listed on pages 57 and 58).

Our favorite kind of research involves talking with planetologists about what they love best—the work they are doing to discover more about our solar system and the universe. We would especially like to thank our editor Tara Moncrief and Sam Storch, Lecturer at the American Museum-Hayden

Planetarium, who reviewed the manuscript and made many excellent suggestions.

—*Ray Spangenburg and Kit Moser*

Index

Numbers in *italics* indicate illustrations.

About the Authors

Ray Spangenburg and Kit Moser write together about science and technology. This husband-and-wife writing team has written 38 books and more than 100 articles. Their works include a five-book series on the history of science and a series on space exploration and astronomy. Their writing has taken them on some great adventures. They have flown on NASA's Kuiper Airborne Observatory (a big plane carrying a telescope). They have also visited the Deep Space Network in the Mojave Desert, where signals from spacecraft are collected. They have even flown in zero gravity on an experimental NASA flight. Ray and Kit live and write in Carmichael, California, with their two dogs, Mencken (a Sharpei mix) and F. Scott Fitz (a Boston Terrier).